MAKING
Bread

MAKING
Bread

DISCARD

RUTH THOMSON
PHOTOGRAPHY: CHRIS FAIRCLOUGH

FRANKLIN WATTS
LONDON/NEW YORK/SYDNEY/TORONTO

Copyright © 1987 Franklin Watts

Franklin Watts Inc
387 Park Avenue South
New York, N.Y. 10016

US ISBN: 0–531–10422–7
Library of Congress Catalog
Card No: 87–50451

Printed in Belgium

Design: Edward Kinsey
Illustrations: Kathleen McDougall

The publisher, author and
photographer would like to
thank Aubrey Karn of Fieldside
Bakery, Elstead, England, for his
help in the preparation of this
book.

CONTENTS

TAKE A CLOSER LOOK

Bread is one of our most important foods and also one of the oldest foods known. You probably eat it as part of every meal.

Think of all the dozens of kinds of breads there are to choose from. They include white, whole wheat, French, Italian, Jewish, Russian, pumpernickel, rye, pita, salt-rising, corn and many other breads. Some breads are made with raisins, syrup, honey, molasses, milk, fruit, malt, cheese and onion. There are also rolls, bagels, croissants and muffins. Can you think of any others?

▽ Bread is a nourishing food, which provides us with energy, protein, minerals and fiber.

Whatever its shape, size and color, the basic ingredients of bread are the same. Flour, yeast, salt, fat and water are mixed together to form a dough, which is then shaped and baked.

Most bakers use flour made from wheat grain, which is ground into a fine powder. People also grind the grain of rye, corn or sorghum to make flour.

The yeast makes the bread light and airy. It is a living plant which, when mixed with warm water, makes bubbles of gas. This gas makes the bread rise. In India, parts of Africa and the Middle East, people eat flat, or unleavened, bread which does not contain yeast. It is dense and heavy.

△ The basic ingredients for bread are 1. salt and fat 2. yeast 3. water 4. flour.

Wheat
Sorghum
Rye

7

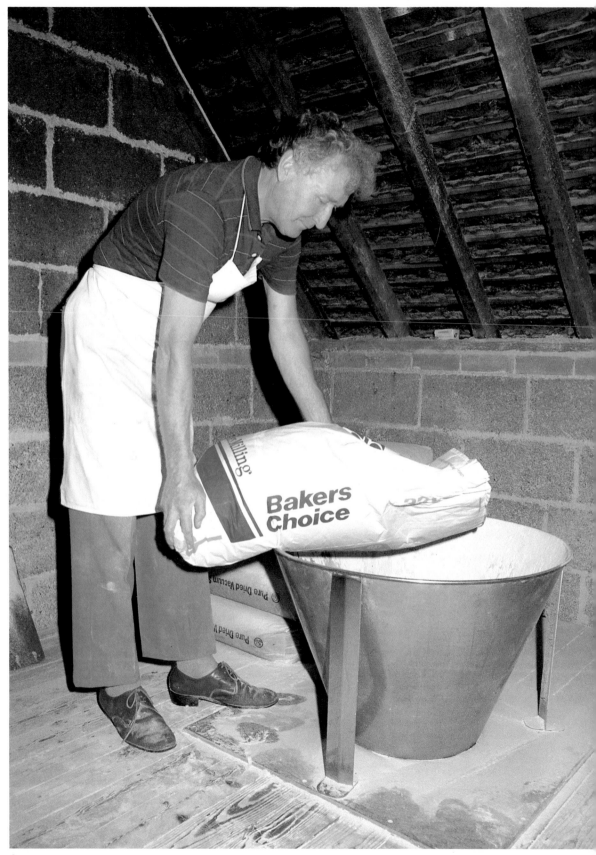

8

MAKING THE DOUGH

Sacks of flour are kept in toreroom above the kery. Flour is tipped wn a huge funnel into a xing bowl below.

Mr Karn buys fresh yeast ch week and keeps it frigerated until he needs use it.

Mr. Karn has been a baker for over forty years. Each weekday, he is up at 4:30 A.M. to bake the day's batch of bread and cakes. On Saturdays, when there is extra demand, he starts work at 1:30 A.M.

To save time in the mornings, Mr. Karn measures out the flour for the next day's baking in the afternoon before. He pours it down a chute, into a dough mixer. He adds measured amounts of salt and fat. The following morning, he weighs the yeast and crumbles it into tiny pieces.

Finally, he adds water to the bowl, after whisking the yeast into it. The temperature of the water he uses depends upon the weather. In hot weather, he uses water from the cold tap. In cold weather, warm water is used instead.

When the machine is turned on, the dough hook turns around and around, mixing the ingredients into a smooth, soft dough. This takes about ten minutes.

Mr. Karn stops the machine once to feel the dough. He can tell, by experience, whether he needs to add more water to the mixture. He scrapes the sides of the bowl to stop the dough from sticking.

Once the dough is mixed, it is left for an hour, while the yeast starts to work.

△ Water is measured out into a bucket.

◁ A huge machine mixes the flour, yeast, salt, fat and water.

▷ When the dough is fully mixed, it can be easily carried. Notice the end of the flour chute above Mr Karn's head.

The cells of yeast start to give off bubbles of carbon dioxide gas, which make the dough expand. Mr. Karn puts a thermometer into the dough. The temperature of the dough rises as the yeast does its work. After an hour, it has risen to 78°F.

Mr. Karn cuts pieces which are the right weight to make a loaf. Finished loaves must weigh a certain weight, according to their size. A weights and measures inspector makes regular visits to bakeries, to check that loaves are the correct weight for their size.

△ A thermometer is pushed into the dough to measure its temperature.

▷ The dough is cut into different size pieces according to the type of bread to be made.

because Mr. Karn is an experienced baker, he can cut pieces that are virtually the right weight. All the same, he puts each piece on the scales to check its weight and adds or removes a bit of dough when necessary. The amount of dough cut for each loaf is heavier than the eventual weight of the finished loaf. This is because a loaf loses weight during baking, as the moisture in it is driven off by the heat of the oven. To make a loaf weighing 24 oz (800 g), Mr. Karn cuts a 28 oz (950 g) piece of dough.

△ The dough for a loaf must weigh exactly the right amount.

The dough is kneaded to balls using the heel of the hand.

Mr Karn kneads some of the pieces, by hand, into balls. Kneading breaks any enormous gas bubbles in the dough, which might otherwise leave big holes when the bread is baked. This is called handing-up.

He puts the balls, quite widely spaced, on a floured wooden tray and covers them with a cotton cloth. The cloth helps both to keep the dough warm (since yeast can only work in the warm) and to prevent a skin from forming on the outside of the balls.

The dough is covered with a cloth and left for about an hour to rise.

The dough is left to rise. This process is called proving. Once the dough has proved, it is ready to be shaped into loaves.

The risen dough is dropped into a machine which molds it into long "sausages."

Dough for making most loaves is shaped in an automatic molding machine. Mr. Karn drops a piece of dough into a feeder at the top of the machine. The dough is carried on a conveyor belt between moving rollers. These squash and shape it into a long flat "sausage," which drops into a trough.

Mr. Karn puts each sausage into a greased loaf tin. He covers the tins with a cotton cloth and leaves the dough to prove yet again.

The tins are greased all over with oil.

When the dough is put into the tins, it only half-fills them at first.

▷ Cottage loaves are hand-moulded. Mr Karn divides a ball of dough so that one piece is twice as big as the other. He rolls them both into balls. He flattens the top of the larger one and presses the smaller ball on top. He makes a deep hole in the top with his thumb and cuts slashes all the way round both pieces.

▷ Plaits are hand-molded as well. Mr. Karn splits a ball into three equal sized pieces and rolls them into long sticks. He then plaits these sticks, just as you might braid wool or hair, pressing them together at the ends. Finally, he sprinkles poppyseed over the top for decoration.

◁ Bloomers are molded by machine but Mr. Karn has to give them a final molding by hand. He cuts several slashes across the top before baking, so that the loaves will "bloom" or rise better. Since they are not baked in tins, the loaves have a crispy crust all over.

▽ Dough is made into many shapes and sizes.

Germ

Endosperm

Bran

▽ Brown bread dough is much coarser in texture than white bread dough.

Mr. Karn does not make only white bread, he also makes wholemeal and brown bread using different types of flour.

Wholemeal flour is made by grinding the whole wheat grain. This is made up of the bran (the skin), the germ (the part from which a new plant will grow) and the endosperm (the inside). Wholemeal flour is the most nutritious kind of flour because none of the goodness of the grain is lost in milling.

Brown flour is made with all the endosperm, but only some of the bran and germ.

White flour is made entirely from the endosperm. Vitamins and minerals are often added to it to make up for what has been lost in milling.

Wholemeal and brown dough are made in a similar way to white dough but the look and the texture differ.

▽ The dough must also be kneaded before being put into tins and allowed to rise.

BAKING THE BREAD

After an hour or so, the dough has risen right to the top of the tins. The loaves are now ready to be baked.

Sandwich loaf tins have a lid on them. This helps to make the shape of the finished loaves as square as possible and ensures that the top of the loaves does not become too brown and crispy during baking. Mr Karn slashes the tops of the other tin loaves with a sharp knife.

He puts the tins into the oven with a long-handled wooden tool called a peel.

▷ The tins are packed in an oven which has three separate compartments.

▽ The dough more than doubles its size in the tin during the rising process.

22

The tins are lifted out of e oven two at a time.

The loaves are baked for about forty minutes. As the heat of the oven cooks the dough, so it also kills the yeast and drives off the bubbles of gas. However, the tiny holes where the gas was remain. If you look closely at a slice of bread, you will see them.

When the loaves are ready, Mr Karn lifts the trays and tins out with the peel. He tips the loaves into a wire tray to cool. He stacks the tins upside-down in a pile.

Now you can see why tin loaves are crispy and browned only on the top and not on the sides.

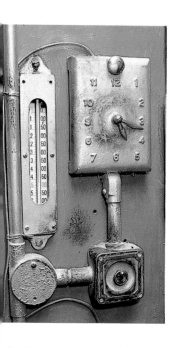

A thermometer shows e temperature of the en, which is usually tween 450–475°F. A ɔck shows the time when e bread will be ready.

Putting the loaves into a re tray allows them to ɔl on all sides at once.

△ Many types of loaves including cottage loaves and bloomers are also baked on flat trays.

◁ Sandwich rolls are bake[d] in tins with lids.

▷ Rolls are baked on flat trays.

READY FOR SALE

The bread is arranged on [the] shelves according to its [siz]e and type.

The trays of bread are wheeled from the bakery into the shop. Mr. Karn times his baking with great precision, so that the first batch of bread is ready at 8:30 AM, when the shop opens.

His work for the day is not over. For the rest of the morning he will bake more bread, cakes, rolls and any special orders. He will clean the bakery so that it is spotless, grease the baking tins and measure out the flour for tomorrow.

White loaves are usually [the] most popular type of [bre]ad.

Mr. Karn enjoys his work. He says there is always something new to learn and that each day's baking is different.

THE PROCESS AT A GLANCE

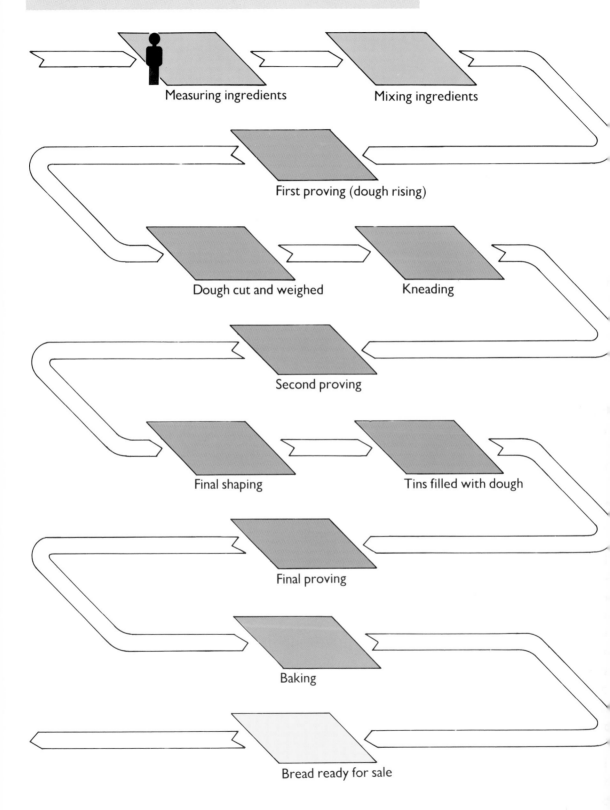

Measuring ingredients

Mixing ingredients

First proving (dough rising)

Dough cut and weighed

Kneading

Second proving

Final shaping

Tins filled with dough

Final proving

Baking

Bread ready for sale

he baking industry serves daily need in almost every ommunity in developed ations. Production is sually highly mechanized. the United States, ommercial bakeries roduce more than 95% of l bread eaten. The baking dustry is one of the largest od-processing industries the United States.

he most popular type of read in the United States white open-top pan read which accounts for at ast 80% of all bread roduction.

he United States Food and rug Administration aintain standards for kery products. White read has strict amounts of quired and optional gredients.

most all White bread ld in the United States is riched. Vitamins and iron ere first added to bread d flour in 1941 as a easure to improve the ation's health. Federal andards today require at enriched bread ontains not less than 11 mg thiamin, 0.7 mg of boflavin, 10 mg of niacin d 8 mg of iron to the und.

Some types of bread

American White bread. A highly porous, commercial loaf made from refined wheat flour. It is usually sold pre-sliced and wrapped.

Barrel. Baked in a corrugated, hinged tin to give a fluted cylindrical shape.

Danish. Open baked loaf with a heavy dusting of flour and with one deep cut across the top.

Bloomer. Long loaf with rounded ends. The top is slashed several times before baking so that the loaf can "bloom" up or rise better.

Cob. A round loaf which can have a sprinkling of crushed wheat on top.

Coburg. A dome shaped loaf baked on the oven bottom.

Rye bread. Usually made from part rye and part wheat flours. Caramel colouring and caraway seeds are often added.

Pumpernickel. A dark, rough and close-textured bread made from cracked or ground whole rye kernels.

French stick. Long thin baton, thick crisp crust with or without poppy seeds, at its best a few hours after baking.

Poppy seed plait. Very crusty braided loaf decorated with poppy seeds.

Farmhouse. Baked in a tin with the rounded corners, dusted with flour and cut down the center before baking.

Salt-rising bread. A Midwestern American loaf with a slightly sour taste, made by allowing corn-meal batter to ferment with wild yeast spores.

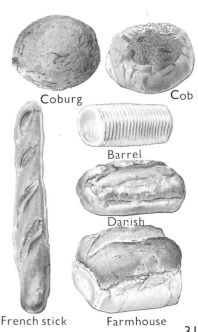

Coburg

Cob

Barrel

Danish

French stick

Farmhouse

INDEX

PRINTED IN BELGIUM BY
proost
INTERNATIONAL BOOK PRODUCTION